Holding You, Holding Me

Whisper's of Mother's Heart

NIDHI SHAH

BookLeaf Publishing

India | USA | UK

Made with ❤ on the BookLeaf Publishing Platform
www.bookleafpub.in
www.bookleafpub.com

Dedication

To my Precious daughter, Viyaana

Your every tiny giggle, all those sleepless nights, every hug reminds me there is no limit to my love for you. You are the poetry that my heart never knew it could write. In your laughter, I hear music; in your embrace, I find home.

May you always know how deeply you are loved, how fiercely you are cherished. This book is for you because you are my forever inspiration

Preface

One day when you are old enough to read this by yourself, I want you to know how deeply you are loved from the very beginning of being in my tummy. This book is my way of holding onto the magic of our time together - the sleepy cuddles, the laughs, your every first moments that are captured in my heart.

For you, Here I am just trying to share part of my feelings of motherhood Joy and embracing every tiny little detail about you. It is filled with moments of quiet beauty and overwhelming chaos, of laughter and tears, of strength discovered in the depths of vulnerability. This book is a collection of those moments, captured in verse.

When I became a mother, I found myself searching for words to express the emotions that surged through me. The indescribable joy, the aching fears, the small victories that felt like the biggest triumphs. Poetry became my refuge, my way of making sense of the whirlwind that is motherhood. Every sleepless night, every whispered lullaby, every tiny hand reaching for mine held a story waiting to be told.

This book is for every mother who has ever felt unseen,

every parent who has questioned if they are enough, and
every heart that has been changed by the incredible
journey of nurturing a child. Whether you are in the
throes of new motherhood, watching your children grow
too quickly, or simply reflecting on the love of a mother,
I hope these words find a home in your heart.

May these poems remind you that in all the mess, magic,
and mayhem, you are not alone.

Acknowledgements

This book is a labor of love, and I could not have written it without the support, wisdom, and love of those who have walked this journey with me.

First and foremost, to my precious Daughter—you are the inspiration behind every word. Your presence in my life has filled my heart with a love so deep, so unconditional, that it overflows onto these pages. You are my greatest teacher, my greatest joy, and my forever blessing.

To my family, thank you for your encouragement, your guidance, and your unwavering support. Your words of wisdom, late-night conversations, and helping hands have made this journey even more beautiful.

To all the mothers—past, present, and future—this book is for you. Motherhood is a journey of love, sacrifice, and resilience, and I honor each of you for the incredible strength you carry every day.

And finally, to my own mother—your love and sacrifices have shaped the mother I am today. Your example of unconditional love has guided me in ways I never fully understood until now.

This book is a reflection of love, growth, and the unbreakable bond between a mother and her child. Thank you to everyone who has been a part of this journey. I am forever grateful.

With love and gratitude,
Nidhi

1. CARRYING LOVE

The day I conceived I carried more than just a Baby,
I carried Love, Holding tight

I heard a tiny heartbeat soft and new,
I felt a dream unfolding so Pure and true.

Within me grew a world so small,
yet filled with wonder, controlling me all.

Little kicks felt so bright
a whispered promise in the night.

Through sleepless nights, I carry hope,
Through clucless days I carry light.

Each breath I take, you take it too
makes me wonder how magical are you.

One day, my arms will hold you near,
But for now, you're safely here.

Nestled close, beneath my heart,
Together still never apart.

I carry love, I always will,
My mom heart is never still.

2. THE JOURNEY EATHSIDE-Delivering My Love

The day you arrived the world stood still,
the air felt so light & heart to thrill.

Through waves of time I whispered a prayer,
I held my breath you were almost there.

I felt scared with hopeful eyes,
I met my heart beneath the skies.

A breath so new, bathed in hue,
A whisper of hope, turns so true.

The cry that fills the silent night,
A brand new soul, pure & bright.

Softest whispers with fleeting pain,
Love poured down like a gentle rain.

The wait ends and the journey starts,
A tiny soul to fill our hearts.

A mother's breath & father's hands
a love that time itself withstands.

3. FIRST BREATH FOREVER
LOVE-early days

The newborn days, a tender phase,
A lifetime starts in tiny ways.

A whispered gasp, so faint, so true,
Yet in that sound, my soul just knew.

A precious life that softly grows,
With tiny hands and tiny toes.

In every cry a comfort found,
with every hug a heart unbound.

Eyes that blink, trying to see,
A brand-new world, so wild and free.

Tiny hands that grasp and hold,
A love so deep, a heart of gold.

From the first coo to the sleepy smile,

Each moment's magic, each step worthwhile.

No greater gift, no sight so bright,
Than you for arriving in my light.

In every feed I promise to keep,
The warmth between us, pure & deep.

4. SWADLLING A DREAM
0-3Months journey

A little soul, a comfort found,
in swaddled arms, love is bound.

With every yawn, with every cry,
A new adventure begins to fly.

Softest fingers, curling tight,
Reaching out in dawn's first light.

Heartbeat whispers, hush and sway,
Rocking time in love's ballet.

First a flutter, then a gaze,
Eyes like stars in newborn haze.

Your first three months, a gift untold,
A love more precious than pure gold.

Each little hum , each sleepy stare,

Tells us you're growing, here and there.

Three small months, yet worlds have spun,
A journey bright, just begun.

Wrapped in love, swaddled you stay,
My baby dreams the night away.

5. MILESTONES OF MAGIC- 3-6months journey

At three to six, you start to bloom,
With every giggle, you light the room.

Tiny feet & chubby hands,
In this age your world expands.

From rolling over to sitting tall,
You're growing up, so proud, so small.

That first smile, that sweetest laugh,
made me wonder how cute you are.

You giggle, you coo, you start to play,
A brand-new person, every day.

From tiny babbles to playful kicks,
You're learning fast with every fix.

The first six months, a lovely start,

With every beat, you steal our heart.

The milestones come, the time flies quick,
you stole my heart in every beat.

6. FROM CRAWLS TO CLAPS- 6-9months journey

The first crawl, slow and small,
a baby on hands & knees wondering all.

Exploring every detail inch by inch,
with the eyes that never really finch.

At six to nine, you start to shine,
With little hands that gently climb.

Life taught you lessons with every wiggle & reach
Each tiny movement, a lesson to preach

Then one day, with joy, you stop,
And with bright eyes, you start to clap and hop.

First clapping hands, then bouncing feet,
Each little leap, a new heartbeat.

With every step and every smile,
You make each moment so worthwhile.

12

7. FROM WOBBLES TO WONDERS-The last strech before 1

Just 9 months & oh so bright,
Growing fast full of light.

A tiny voice, a perfect sound,
"Mumma" sounded so profound.

A single word so delight,
no other sweeter sound in my mind.

From babbling hums to words so clear,
Your little voice, I'll always hear.

At ten months, a wobbly stand,
Tiny fingers clutching a hand.

A shaky step & another try,
Wide-eyed wonder, reaching high.

In moments quiet, in moments loud,
You will be one, above the crowd.

But nothing else will touch my soul,
Like "Mumma" first my heart made whole.

8. ONE YEAR, ONE WONDER- 12months old

One year, one wonder, love so true,
A gift the world received in you.

Twelve bright moons have lit your way,
From newborn cries to laughs that stay.

Through every moment, joy has grown,
And how fast the time has flown.

One year ago, you came to be,
A tiny dream, a mystery.

With eyes so wide and hands so small,
You filled our hearts & had it all.

Twelve sweet months, how fast they flew,
Filled with love and dreams brand new.

The softest whispers, the warmest touch,
Oh, little one, you mean so much!

16

9. BETWEEN LOVE & EXHAUSTION- The silent battle

Motherhood is a journey of boundless love and relentless sacrifice, a delicate balance between devotion and exhaustion. From the moment I wake up, my world revolves around tiny hands that need me, yet in giving so much, I often forget myself. The sleepless nights, the aching body, the unspoken loneliness, these battles remain unseen. I have smiled through the fatigue, carried the weight of expectations, and pushed forward even when my strength felt depleted. The world sees the love, but not always the struggle. Yet, through the exhaustion, I remained unwavering, my heart kept beating not just for myself but for the little soul I nurture. Though I bend, I do not break, because a mother's love, though heavy, is the strongest force of all. I love my child with all my heart does not change the fact that I don't miss my life and work before having a baby so here I'm just sharing a part of motherhood which every mom goes through but feels unheard. I myself have people telling me you have been working for so many years and now just don't sit at home and only be obsessed with your baby, Do something, but guess what here I am with almost a 2-year old giving her my complete devotion so she is raised just like how I want her to raise and not by anyone else. So below there is a little struggle of every new Mom, who loved their babies more than themselves but also do miss the early phase.

She gave the world a brand-new light,
Yet feels herself fade into night.

A body changed, a mind unsure,
A love so deep, but wounds so pure.

The mirror shows a face she knew,
But shadows whisper, "Is that you?"

The sleepless nights, the aching frame,
The heart that loves but feels the strain.

The world says, *"Joy! This time is sweet."*
But no one sees she's lost beneath,

Beneath the weight, the endless call,
Of giving more, of giving all.

She longs for rest, a gentle hand,
For someone else to understand.

Yet in the dark, she fights, she stays,
Through weary nights and endless days.

For who she was, for sleep she craves,
For freedom lost in tidal waves.

And though she bends, she does not break,
She is the dawn, she is awake.

10. JUST A MOM–YET EVERYTHING

She wakes before the world can see,
With sleepy eyes and love so free.

She ties small shoes and wipes each tear,
She calms their cries, she chases fear.

She folds the clothes, she sings the songs,
She holds them close where they belong.

She gives her time, she gives her all,
She picks them up when they feel small.

Through endless days and fleeting years,
She hides her worries, swallows her tears.

But in their laughter, in their cheer,
She finds her strength, her purpose clear.

She needs no crown, no grand applause

She's just a mom, and that's enough.

No medal shines upon her chest,
But in their hearts, she is the best.

For though the world may not quite see,
She builds their home, their memories.

No need for fame, no grand applause
She's just a mom, and that's enough.

11. THE HEART THAT HOLDS IT ALL

Her laughter rings like morning light,
Her arms, a home so warm & bright.

Through tiny hands and little feet,
Her love makes every day complete.

She sings, she dances, spins around,
Turns teardrops into joy profound.

She lifts them high, she lets them grow,
Yet in her heart, they'll always glow.

She carries dreams, she spreads her wings,
She builds a world where love still sings.

No matter big, no matter small,
She has a heart that holds it all.

Through every fall, through every fight,

She stands, she stays, she is their light.

No thanks she asks, no rest she seeks,
Her love speaks loud when words are weak.

And though the years may steal her prime,
Her love will stand the test of time.

For even when they're grown and tall,
She'll be the heart that holds it all.

12. THE ROAD WE WALK TOGETHER

We walk through fields, through sunshine's glow,
She stops to watch the flowers grow.

She jumps in puddles, spins with cheer,
I hold her close, I keep her near.

Her little hands reach up so high,
"Mom, don't let go," she whispers with Sigh.

She stumbles once, I lift her high,
I wipe her tears, I hush her shy

But time moves fast, like fleeting days,
Her little feet will find their way.

And though she'll walk a path brand new,
She'll always know, I'm walking too.

No matter where, no matter when,

She'll turn and find me there again.

For through this life, in any weather,
This road is ours we walk together.

Through every joy, through every steer
This road is ours we walk together.

13. BLOOMING IN LOVE

Like petals unfurling in morning light,
A mother and daughter hearts woven tight.

Rooted in kindness, watered with grace,
Their love blossoms in time and space.

Lessons whispered, laughter shared,
A bond so deep, none compared.

The mother, strong like an ancient tree,
The daughter, a bud so wild and free.

Yet side by side, they grow as one,
Blooming in love, like earth and sun.

No wind can break, no time erase,
The bond we share, the love we trace.

For in each bloom, a story told,
Of love so pure, forever gold.

14. HELD BY LOVE, SURROUNDED BY MOMMY

A Poem through my daughter's eyes.

The world is big, but I am small,
Yet in your arms, I have it all.

Your hands are soft, your touch so light,
You hold me close all through the night.

The sky may stretch so wide and free,
But all I need is you and me.

The sun may shine, the stars may glow,
But in your love, I truly grow.

No place too far, no dream too tall,
With you, Mommy, I have it all.

When I am scared or when I fall,
She lifts me up, she's there through all.

The trees may sway, the rivers run,
The stars may shine, the moon may hum,

But in her hug, so snug, so tight,
I have my world, I have my light.

No need to search, no need to roam,
For Mommy's love is always home.

The stars may twinkle, high and free,
But you're the brightest light to me.

For in my world, both big and small,
You are the greatest love of all.

15. TOY CASTLES & PAINTED DREAMS

Scattered blocks and teddy bears,
Tiny hands that lift with care.

Dolls and cars, a make-believe ride,
Endless joy with you by my side.

Teddy bears and bunnies bright,
Keeping close through day and night.

Brushes dipped in colors bright,
Swirls of wonder, pure delight.

Rainbows bloom on paper wide,
Dreams take shape, side by side.

Laughter spills like drops of gold,
Stories painted, tales retold.

Jumping, dancing, tumbling 'round,

Giggles light up all the ground.

In their arms, no fear, no fray,
Just love and laughter in our play.

Through every game, through every hue,
I find the world in shades of you.

16. MOM & ME, A STORY OF US

Tiny hands, a messy grin,
Mommy's laughter tucked within.

A little chef on tippy toes,
Flour-dusted, button nose.

Morning sunlight fills the air,
Flour dust floats everywhere.

A tiny chef in apron small,
Mixing, stirring, spills and all.

Click A picture while fingers sticky,
Stirring batter, slow but tricky.

Giggling as the cookies bake,
Making memories we won't forsake.

Enjoying the pancakes flip,

Baby touches a frosting dip.

Bath-time bubbles, splashes bright,
Wrapped in towels, hugged so tight.

Building castles, chasing light,
Holding hands from day to night.

Dancing barefoot, twirling free,
Mommy, baby just you and me.

One day soon, you'll spread your wings,
But these sweet days will always cling.

Bedtime stories whispered between yawns,
Drifting to sleep as the moonlight dawns.

Sealed in photos, held so dear,
A treasure of moments crystal clear.

17. PARK TO SHORE, PLAY SOME MORE

Little feet run, fast and free,
Chasing the leaves beneath the trees.

Slides that sparkle in the sun,
Tumbles, giggles & endless fun.

The park is buzzing, swings in flight,
Push me, Mommy, Hold on tight.

Up so high, arms open wide,
Like a bird, she soars with pride.

Hand in hand, we leave the park,
To where the ocean waves embark.

Sandbox castles, little hands,
Building dreams in golden sands.

Cool salt air, toes in tide,

Drifting where the dreams reside.

Buckets filled with shells and sand,
Traces of joy left on the land.

Jumping waves, splashing free,
Running, twirling by the sea.

Shells are gathered, footprints fade,
Memories in the sand are made.

One more game, one more run,
Park to shore, our day is not done.

In every splash, in every cheer,
I hold these moments, forever near.

18. UNTIL MY LAST BREATH- A PROMISE

The moment I saw you, my heart understood,
A love so fierce, so deep & good.

Your fingers curled tightly around my own,
A love like no other, a bond carved in stone.

Through sleepless nights and bright morning beams,
I've watched over you, through laughter and dreams.

Your giggles, your cries, your small hands in mine,
Each moment, a treasure, each second, divine.

I'll guide you with patience, with warmth, and with
grace,
Wipe every tear, kiss each frown from your face.

Through all of your triumphs, through struggles and
fears,
I'll stand by your side for all of your years.

As years may pass, and seasons change,
Through life's winds, however strange,

Know that my love will never fade,
A promise kept, never delayed.

And when my hair turns silver-grey,
When time has taken youth away,

Know, my love, through life and death,
I'll love you still, till my last breath.

No force in this world, not even in death,
Can stop me from loving you till my last breath.

19. MOM, NOW I KNOW! BECOMING A MOM, BECOMING LIKE YOU

A tribute to my own Mom,

Mom, I've said "I love you" before,
But now, those words mean so much more.

The hands that held me, soft & strong,
The voice that guided all along.

The lessons whispered, the sacrifices made,
In your love, I was gently swayed.

The love you gave, so pure & true,
I finally feel it because now, I do too.

Now, as I hold my child so tight,
I understand your quiet might.

The endless patience, the silent care,
The way you were always there.

So, thank you, Mom, for all you've done,
For every hug, for every sun.

I walk your path, I trace your way,
And love my child more each day.

I see your strength in ways I missed,
In every hug, in every kiss.

The worries hidden, the burdens small,
You carried them, I see them all.

And now, as I rock my little one tight,
I feel your love in the softest light.

The circle turns, the love remains,
A mother's heart never wanes.

So thank you, Mom, for all you've done,
For every tear, for every sun.

Because of you, I've come to see
A mother's love lives endlessly.